Letters to Myself
Volume 5
LGBTQIA+, Parental Estrangement & Parental Alienation

By:
Award Winning
&
#1 International Bestselling Author
Jen Taylor, LCSW

ELITE PUBLISHING
HOUSE
YOUR LEGACY. YOUR BOOK.

ELITE PUBLISHING HOUSE
YOUR LEGACY. YOUR BOOK.

First Edition

Copyright 2024 © Jen Taylor, LCSW

All Rights Reserved

No part of this book may be reproduced or transmitted in any form or by any means, electronic or mechanical, including photocopying, recording or by an information storage and retrieval system – except by a reviewer who may quote brief passages in a review to be printed in a magazine, newspaper or on the Web – without permission in writing from the publisher.

Cover Graphics: Kathryn Denhof
Photo Credit: Unknown

To my dear friend, Dinesh, for always believing in me and guiding me through some of the darkest times in my life.

Thank you for the gift that you are in my life.

United States:

If you or someone you know is experiencing a mental health, suicide crisis, or emotional distress, reach out 24/7 to the 988 Suicide and Crisis Lifeline (formerly known as the National Suicide Prevention Lifeline) by dialing or texting 988 or using chat services at suicidepreventionlifeline.org to connect to a trained crisis counselor.

Please see Appendix Suicide Resources for Worldwide Numbers

LGBTQIA+:

https://glaad.org/resourcelist/

https://www.thetrevorproject.org/resources/

https://lgbthotline.org/

https://itgetsbetter.org/

https://gaycenter.org

https://www.gmhc.org

transgenderlawcenter.org

Parental Estrangement:

https://lifestance.com

https://locator.apa.org/

NAMI Helpline (National Alliance on Mental Illness)

1-800-950-6264

TABLE OF CONTENTS

INTRODUCTION 9

COLLECTION OF LETTERS 13

   PART 1: LGBTQIA+

   Anonymous

   Meredith Linden

   M. LaRae, M.Sc.

   Poppy DeKenney

   PART 2: Parental Estrangement

   Anonymous

    Singha

   Elizabeth Myers

   PART 3: Parental Alienation

   Jayson Fieldings, Sr

APPENDIX ON SUPPORT RESOURCES & CHOICES 75

   Includes Links, Numbers, & Resources for LGBTQIA+, Parental Estrangement, and Parental Alienation

APPENDIX ON SUICIDE RESOURCES 75

   Includes Resources for Suicide Help & Assessment

CONDUCT A SUICIDE INQUIRY 90

DETERMINE RISK LEVEL.. 93

ABOUT THE AUTHOR.. 95

INTRODUCTION

When I was 8, I visited my eldest brother at college. He is roughly ten years older than me, making him about 17/18 at the time – in the early 1970s. I remember seeing a man who passed by, dressed all in black leather and commenting to my brother that he must be gay. My brother took this opportunity to educate me about the fact that not all gay men dress the same and that he, himself, was gay. I remember being a little surprised but not shocked. My response was that I always knew there was something different about him. That was the gift my brother gave me by trusting my eight-year-old self to accept and honor who he was. I did, and I still do. In doing so, he allowed me to open my perspective about what "normal" was. I guess I can rephrase that and say that being gay was just another part of one of the people I loved most in my life. That allowed me to be more accepting and inclusive of others from a young age. Fifty years later, being part of the gay community is more accepted, and gay marriage is legal in The United States of America and many other countries.

I believe strongly that my brother's openness about his gay identity and my upbringing by my middle-class, grassroots, liberal parents began to carve out the identity of who I am today and what brings me to publish this volume focusing on LGBTQIA+ stories. My parents were from two vastly different cultures; my mother was the daughter of Jewish

Odessan immigrants fleeing the Russian pogroms in the early 1900s. My father was raised Southern Baptist in Alabama and then converted when he met my mother in order to raise our family Jewish. When my father first met my maternal grandmother, the story goes that my Nana said, "John, this has never happened in my family," to which he responded, "Rose, I can assure you, this has never happened in my family!" "This," being intermarriage. They became "fast friends," as my mother would say.

An inherent part of who I am involves accepting others as they are. My goal in my therapy work is to help others be their authentic selves, whatever that may include.

Parental estrangement:

A part of this volume is dedicated to individuals who have experienced parental estrangement, either from their own parents or by their children. There was a time when coming out as gay or lesbian often coincided with parental estrangement due to a lack of acceptance of their child's identity. Some parents have been estranged by their children. The pain from both can be excruciating, and parents may often ask themselves what they have done wrong or where they have fallen short. If the family member is open to attending therapy together, I would say go for it! If not, my suggestion is to do your own inventory. If there is something you feel you have done wrong as a parent, apologize to your kid. It may also be the other person's issue, although often both parties hold some responsibility.

Parental alienation:

Parental alienation is " a situation in which one parent uses strategies – sometimes referred to as brainwashing, alienating, or programming – to distance a child from the other parent." - Healthline.

That may involve discrediting the other parent to the child, telling the child that the other parent is "bad" or doesn't love them. This behavior can alter the child's perspective of the other parent and create an alienated relationship. I know a few people who have experienced this and am aware of how painful this can be. There is hope that things can change, as our author, Jayson, recounts in his story.

COLLECTION OF LETTERS

Part One:

LGBTQIA+

Dear Young Self, on the verge of coming out,

I know you're terrified because you feel you can't go backward and you're afraid to go forward. I understand completely. I'm writing to tell you this: Move ahead. It will be awful at times, but more often it will be great. You can't imagine the life you're going into because it hasn't happened yet; because it's nothing like the life you've had up until now; because the world is going to be changing in ways you do not expect and cannot know. But I can tell you this: it's going to be good.

I know you. You're afraid to come out because all you know about being gay are the few things you've read, a couple of movies that made you worry, and a boy who never loved you as much as you loved him. That was hard, harder than it should have been. He wasn't kind to you, that boy, but it wasn't because of you: it was because he didn't really love himself. You'll discover, over time, that his life is not better than yours, that he's not better than you—not better looking, not more successful, not happier. And what you don't know, even now, is how much he looks up to you. You'll find that out, one day, but for now just trust me: it's true.

Looking back from what is for you many years in the future, I can tell you the things you'll love about being gay. You'll meet truly interesting people, of all kinds. The gay world is smaller than the straight world, but as a result it's much more diverse, and other gay people are more open to you because you have something in common. In some ways you'll be an outsider, but because of that you'll have a better perspective on reality. You'll gain access to a world of art and literature that you'd otherwise be a stranger to, and you'll be far more creative yourself.

You're worried about not being respectable anymore. This, too, is a misjudgment. You'll be astonished to see how normal being gay will become in the years to come. You'll tell everyone you're gay, and you won't lose friends or jobs or income. And you won't be unsafe: nobody is going to beat you up, or harass you. Let go of the fear: it's misguided, and you don't need it.

You're afraid you will never find love, but you will. You'll find little bits of it all everywhere—in connecting with strangers, in friendships, in partnerships, and in family. You'll be disappointed at times, sometimes greatly, but that will be because you've misjudged situations, not because the situations themselves are wrong. And people will love you back. You'll have boyfriends, lovers, partners, and even a husband one day. You'll know what it means to be stable and content.

I don't want to give away too many secrets, but one thing I can tell you now is that you won't have children. Surprisingly, many gay people will; friends will. But that's just not on your path in this lifetime. Don't worry; let it go. There will be other joys.

You will not lose family members by coming out. Don't be surprised: they've always loved you, and you've always been gay, since you were born. They'll be fine.

What you will have is comfort, excitement, professional achievement, creativity, travel, faith. You will have people who love you, some more than you will ever know. You won't think you're attractive, but other people will. You'll be funny, and smart, and charming. People will admire you for what you do and like you for who you are. You will learn to cook and write and sing and exercise and plan and manage money and pray.

There will be hard times, no doubt about it, some harder than you could imagine for reasons that don't exist yet. But you will get through them, get stronger, learn how to manage and fight back. And the hardest times will come not from others but from you, from fear and worry and your thoughts. So, here's a message, from me to you: worry less, have more confidence in yourself, more faith. Things really will work out; problems will resolve; good things you can't imagine will come along.

Remember to love yourself more; to enjoy every day; to look on the bright side; and to be grateful for all the good things that you have, both the ones that come to stay and the ones that pass through your life. They're all gifts, as is life itself.

Love,

You

                                                    -Anonymous

I could not explain anything about it while it was happening. I knew, without having had an affair, that I was a lesbian. The years of analyzing almost every dream I have started when I was coming out, trying to figure out if I was really gay or not. In my second year of exploring my sexuality, while married to a man and with two small children, I wrote: "I am beginning to wonder if I will ever feel at peace. Will transition ever end?" My husband and I thought of all kinds of ways to not divorce for two years. I tried so hard to make sense of it all, but it wasn't something to intellectualize. I left it to the Universe, to some degree. SOMETHING was telling me things were going to be okay. But NOTHING was in place. Though life got messy, the things that centered me were knowing I was not heterosexual and my ability to lean into that.

I still have to come out, and I still secret myself as I move in myriad social circles. I maneuver in my own cycles, expanding and contracting as life, safety, and groundedness direct me. I have become much more in tune with the rhythms of ebb and flow, so coming out became less of an event and more of a process.

Recouped

Vitality after the drought
Yields sustenance recouped
The dry spell passes a stone
Drops of blood offer a new tone

Wetting the ears,
Salivating the senses,
As life recouped.
What once was parched,
Cracked and shattered
Teems with juices,
Looses the noose
Of imminent death.
A trickle
Of love recouped,
An open plea refusing to yield,
Speaking the truth
Of passion recouped.

Home

Home in a little pod upon the sea,
She dipped her hand and said to me,
Home is where the heart is
And yours is far away.
Bring it closer still,
Protected from the fray
Of life too much lived
Of crusty shallow breaths,
The kind that cough and spurt,
And offer up a death.
Take note of crests and waves,
She said to me once more,
When water's splashing in your boat
While reaching for the shore,
You'll know a home is one that sticks.
You'll see the smile that you have picked

Matches the one inside.

I am grateful to have had the process of coming out and all it has taught me about life's rhythms and how they impact me. I have learned to gain my strength from the inside and choose when I am out. In 2010, I wrote: I am searching for the balance I can create on my own – inside. How wonderful that in 2024, I can say that I have a much greater ability to create my own balance on a regular basis through the healing I have done and continue to do, which includes continually recognizing my safety needs.

Though I came out in the 1990s (at age 32), I was conditioned by the generational fears and hazards of life before me and in my youth. It seems we have more acceptance, love, and visibility now in some ways, but there is still a way to go. Each human that comes out and shows themselves in all their authenticity is living a life of great courage and bravery. I am proud to be among such warriors.

-Meredith Linden

"True belonging only happens when we present our authentic, imperfect selves to the world. Our sense of belonging can never be greater than our level of self – acceptance." -Brene Brown

The LGBTQ community has been hiding their authentic selves from the world out of actual fear for their lives. Fear of losing their jobs. Fear of losing their families and friends. Fear of being cast out of communities and having to leave their homes. These fears have materialized all too often for many of the human beings who identify as LGBTQ.

Society has forever taunted, tortured, and attacked people in these communities, and far too many times, these situations have ended with fatal consequences.

My daughter was in her senior year of college when she came out to me, and I think we were both surprised about the level of anxiety she felt as she approached the conversation. We both knew that I was completely accepting and yet she still felt nervous and apprehensive. I'm not sure if she was worried about the reaction I would actually have or if she was just anxious that it would create a level of acknowledgment within herself that she could now be visible to the world.

Public visibility for the LGBTQ community carries an elevated risk of danger for them as they go about their everyday lives. Simply living day to day and expressing their authentic self can be full of constant precautions and stress. Activism and support are vital for protecting the rights and lives of the LGBTQ communities and building open discussions that will keep creating a forward movement.

LGBTQ movements date back at least to the 1920s. Fighting for the right to simply be themselves. Fighting to simply live their lives and love who they want legally, socially, and publicly. Fighting for the right to not be an illegal human being. Fighting for the freedom to hold hands in public or go to dinner as a couple in peace without harassment, accusations, or assault. Fighting for the right to simply exist.

Growing up in the 1980s, these so-called "deviant" lifestyles weren't openly discussed most of the time. They were kept hush-hush. Those who were talking were mocking and making fun of people. I think most of us just didn't bring it into our minds or make it part of our open conversations. To speak openly felt taboo and discouraged. We didn't bring those thoughts out into conversations until the aids epidemic thrust the topic wide out into the open.

The aids (acquired immunodeficiency syndrome) epidemic that ramped up in the early 80's struck fear into the hearts of everyday people. Those misinformed fears brought about an intense increase in acts of violence and hate toward gay and lesbian communities. Some people were evicted from their homes by landlords and some were kicked out by family members as well as losing their jobs, and many were also being avoided by the medical providers.

The previous decade had seen an explosion of LGBTQ activism stemming from the Stonewall Uprising in 1969. This was a historic turning point for the gay rights movement. Many activist organizations formed during this time, including PFLAG (Parents, Families, & Friends of Lesbians and Gays). According to pflag.org, they are "the nation's largest organization dedicated to supporting, educating, and advocating for LGBTQ+ people and those who love them."

Then, in 1998, we experienced the tragic death of Matthew Shepard. This senseless and horrific story captivated the world and, I think, began to steer to conversation away from hate and toward understanding and acceptance. His story led to the Hate Crimes Prevention Act. This is legislation signed into law in 2009 to grant more authority to investigate hate crimes and provide funding for the investigations of hate crimes.

Then, in 2016, came the unfathomable Pulse nightclub tragedy that took 49 human beings from this earth and injured many others. This shook every inch of the LGBTQ community with grief. They were simply enjoying their evening. They were simply spending time with friends. They were simply living their lives. They were simply existing authentically in a supposed safe space.

These events and many more pushed forward changes and brought about legislation to protect the gay and lesbian communities, and for that, I am thankful. There is still so much work to do in order to protect our LGBTQ communities.

What should be a basic human right to be married to the person you love and want to share your life with wasn't even legal for the LGBTQ communities until 2015, when the Supreme Court ruled that all states must acknowledge and accept same-sex marriages.

As parents and allies, how do we process and deal with the intentional cruelty leveled at our kids, family members, and friends who are part of these communities? Honestly, sometimes it is emotionally exhausting and too hard to process so much hate, and some days, I feel like a bulldozer ready to run over anyone, blocking their access to freedom, open happiness, and human rights.

I want my daughter to be happy. I want her to feel safe in her community and workplace. I want her to enjoy her life authentically and openly, just like people who are not part of these communities. I want her to not have to worry about who knows and who doesn't. One of my greatest hopes is that we could change society into a space where neither of us has to worry about her safety. We don't completely live in that situation yet, but there are places and spaces that are open and inclusive. Likewise, there are still so many places and spaces that are not safe for LGBTQ.

When young adults are looking to begin their adult lives with work opportunities, many in the LGBTQ community need to evaluate the inclusiveness of the area in which they are contemplating living their lives. Although no place can be assured to be completely safe, it's important to evaluate the level of safety in the area, the community, and surrounding areas.

I think as parents and allies we have to keep talking and sharing inclusive language and opportunities. I think we have to pay attention to bills being introduced into legislation and make sure that rights are not being rescinded. We have to be an open voice of support whenever we can and whenever is needed.

If I could write letters back in time, I may write letters to the people of Stonewall. I would like them to know that we will not give up this fight for acceptance and how sorry I am that people could be so cruel. And that I love them not only just the way they are but especially the way they are.

I would write letters to the aids victims and families telling them I wish more people could be compassionate and understanding. I wish for more people to stand up against the misinformation and hate. And that we will not give up this fight for existence and that I love them.

I would write letters to Matthew Shepard's family expressing my heartfelt sorrow for their grief. And that I wish people didn't have so much hate toward another human being as to commit such a horrific act of violence. And that I love them and Matthew and that we will not give up this fight for existence.

I would like to write a letter to myself asking myself to be aware of the injustice happening around me at an earlier age.

To be aware of the cruelty and inhuman treatment of the LGBTQ communities. To start speaking out and getting involved to change policies and laws so that they are protected and legally empowered to live their lives according to them.

As Brene Brown said in the opening quote about self-acceptance being equal to our level of belonging, I feel we must strive to reinforce the acceptance of the LGBTQ community. We have to make sure that they know without any doubt that they do belong in our communities, they are part of our communities and that we love and support them.

A few resources:

https://www.thetrevorproject.org/resources/

- You can call the LGBT National Hotline at 888-843-4564

- You can call the LGBT National Youth Talkline at 800-246-7743

- You can call the LGBT National Coming Out Support Hotline at 888-688-5428

- You can access the Weekly Youth Chatrooms at lgbthotline.org/youthchatrooms

- Q Chat Space is a bully-free online community of LGBTQ+ teens that can chat with other LGBTQ+ teens and vetted/trained staff from LGBTQ+ community centers around the country. The community is managed by CenterLink.

You can access Q Chat Space at www.qchatspace.org

-*M. LaRae, M.Sc.*

Metaphysician/Reiki Master/Best Selling Author

I always knew I was gay since grade school and many other people knew about it. It wasn't as widely accepted as it is now. I eventually fell in love with a woman who made me happy, and that made me feel that maybe I was just confused and not gay. As we started going to black-tie weddings as a couple and to other family events, I began to feel so normal being with a woman. We eventually got married, but I was still attracted to guys. We eventually divorced for unrelated reasons, and I was never seen again dating a woman. Fast forward three years, I learned about a gay dating website that would let me meet guys for anything from sex to relationships. I sampled a variety of each until I found a significant other and dated for about ten years. Part of that time became a long-distance relationship that became a break-up partly due to the difficulties of maintaining a long-distance relationship. It also did not help that his family was more conservative about homosexuality. I am single now but not necessarily looking for the next available single guy. The important thing is to be happy whether that person is the opposite gender or your own. I'm thankful that my family is accepting of any of the choices that I have made, and I am sorry for those who do not have that same support.

-JB

When I was four, my mom routinely made me take an afternoon nap. One nap was revelatory. I dreamt of walking down a street in my hometown in a bright yellow patent leather minidress and matching platform boots and purse; it was the sixties, after all. I remember feeling extremely contented, even for a time after I awoke. As a child, I routinely played with female friends and cousins, often playing dress-up. This always felt normal and natural. Adults, more often than not, mistook me for a girl. What a cute little girl, they'd exclaim, to quick clarification from either of my parents.

For most of my childhood, I wasn't aware that there were physical differences between boys and girls. In one city we lived in, I had a female friend who lived across the courtyard. She used to love to follow me into the bathroom when I visited her house; at age eleven, she promised to "show me hers if I showed her mine." I resisted, feeling there was something naughty about doing that. She persisted, and I eventually relented. She showed me something, but it was nothing. I was mad for a while, believing she had tricked me and hadn't shown me "hers" at all. But, someday, maybe when science class covered anatomy, I realized she had shown me "hers." When we studied intersexed people in biology, I found myself envious of them. At that time, I was not aware that doctors would often choose a gender at birth and remove the "extra" genitalia.

I began to become increasingly aware I didn't fit. Or that I was broken. I didn't know anyone like me. I hadn't heard about anyone like me. Through my teen years and early phases of adulthood, I just thought I had a kinky side. I worked hard to keep it hidden. Eventually, I learned of Christine Swedishname, an American servicemember who traveled to Sweden, with much controversy, to transition surgically. Then there was Tula, a British transsexual model, famous for her legs on the James Bond For Your Eyes Only movie poster and her 1991 Playboy spread. I thought both looked significantly better as women. But I had repressed my own instincts for so long that neither triggered a connection. In fact, by the time Tula was a public persona, I had discovered sex and was quite happy to be male.

I had a reasonably normal adulthood and marriage until my spouse found photos of me cross-dressing. Before that, I had been successful in hiding. She had a very traditional, conservative upbringing, and the discovery changed our relationship permanently. Eventually, she concluded I must be gay. I tended to concede the point because I really had no context in the mid-1990s other than the gay community. But I was not particularly interested in men. And while I had been to the occasional drag show, I wasn't drawn in that direction either.

Then, in 1998, she asked for a divorce. Not only had she concluded I was gay, she wanted a relationship with a "normal" man. When she asked, she told me she had never wanted children. About six years too late, considering our daughter. Even with the changed relationship, she had been my best friend. So, it was a difficult time.

While living in Boston, I was assigned to work in Manhattan for a few weeks. During that assignment, in a restaurant guide, I saw an ad for a place called Lucky Cheng's, an Asian fusion restaurant. It was famous for its waitresses, all cross-dressed Asian men. I went there, quite terrified, wearing sexy panties and bra under my jeans and tee shirt. I was stunned at how beautiful and completely passable all the women working there were.

The experience at Lucky Cheng's and the increasing ease of information available on the internet encouraged me to start looking for organizations serving people like me. As someone who was uncertain of her identity, gender, and sexuality, I began to research. Initially, it was a slow process, partly because of my fears about where this road would lead me. Online, I found the Human Rights Campaign that broadly served and advocated for the LGBTQIA+ community. I also located the Tiffany Club of New England (TCNE), which specifically served both cross-dressers and transgendered people. When I was growing up, these groups were lumped together, though quite distinct, under the somewhat derogatory term, transvestite. It took two years for me to build the courage to actually call. I would get as nervous as I did in middle school about calling someone I had a crush on. I feared they would indoctrinate me into becoming a woman. This fear insinuated that it would somehow be against my will.

But I eventually reached a point where I knew I had to call, if for no other reason, that the solitude of my condition had become unbearable. I finally went to an open house to learn more about the organization and its events, and shortly after that, I started attending events. I began making friends. My group of friends included both crossdressers and male-to-female transgender people. It didn't take long to realize that, while I enjoyed all my new friends, I gravitated toward transgender people as kindred spirits. It was revelatory and helped me gradually break down my fears and resistance to what I instinctively knew as a child. I had passed a point where there was no turning back. I knew what to do, and those engagements helped prepare me for the difficult road ahead.

I also joined several other groups and began attending events. I went to gay bars, lesbian bars, drag shows, fetish events, and TCNE events. Those experiences helped, through a process of elimination, for me to evolve a better understanding of myself, my needs, and my path toward a fulfilling life. For example, at one LGBT (back then) club, a gorgeous gay dancer working for the club tried to pick me up with the line, "I bet you're really butch as a guy!" I was offended and insulted and realized he simply didn't get it. And as beautiful as he was as a male specimen, I appreciated his beauty (like appreciating Michelangelo's David) but had no interest sexually.

But it was a vital part of the process of elimination. It contributed to that understanding of self. I developed a few infatuations with lesbians I met, but they all proved too concerned about their images with their friends to date a transgender person, whether pre- or post-operative. Again, the process of elimination. The drag shows I attended were barely an amusement. The men enjoyed portraying women in an often amusing or satirical way but had no identification as women. But, again, engaging with multiple potential peer groups allowed me to discover my own identity and understand where I was genuinely comfortable and where I fit.

And where I fit was with the transgender community. Most of my transgender friends were pre-op or non-op, meaning that they hadn't or wouldn't transition surgically. The most common reason that a male-to-female transgender person would not transition surgically was marriage to a supportive spouse who opposed their transition. The other was career or workplace issues. Post-ops generally do not remain in the community. Somewhat sadly, perhaps, most prefer to live a more conventional or "normal" life. It is simply easier, more so today shockingly than 20 or so years ago when I transitioned, to be perceived as a woman wholly or to the extent possible. I thought we were achieving progress, but obviously…

By the time I was ready to confront the transition, I was solidly and happily divorced. My ex quickly remarried to the man she was dating during the period of our divorce. She had long ago moved in him, anyway, and had left my daughter and I largely behind. Though we shared custody, my daughter lived with me, except on the few occasions I had to travel overnight. My daughter lived and was supportive throughout my transition. But it was not easy for her, despite living in a comparatively liberal Massachusetts town.

My family knew well before I even began seriously considering transition. Around the time we separated, my spouse, struggling with my issues, essentially outed me to my parents. Sensing a potential crisis, they came to visit and assess the situation. My dad, often a staunch critic full of advice, was surprisingly supportive (though later, it took him years to adjust to the name and pronoun changes). My mother was a conservative British woman who had always been overly concerned with appearances. She often asked, "What will the neighbors think?" usually, but not always, in jest. But in jest lies truth, so she was more than happy for me to keep this private.

Unlike my trans friends who had workplace issues preventing their transition, I was fortunate to work for the government, which, under republican president George W. Bush, had instituted protections for LGBTQIA+. That doesn't mean it was easy as a result; it just meant even if some might have wanted either to fire me or have me fired.

One lesson I learned in the process is that you never know how people will react. That is probably true any time someone they know or work with transitions or who comes out in any fashion. Few people understood what it meant not to be cisgender, a term few people even knew at the time. Some assumed I suffered from some delusional or even dangerous psychopathy. Face value acceptance was uncertain from person to person. I found it particularly challenging to deal with coworkers and bosses, but surprisingly, friends and neighbors. They often had no basis for understanding my journey. Generally, though, women were much more likely to be supportive or at least understanding and compassionate.

For example, Dana, a male coworker, was a routine pain in my work life. Yet, he was surprisingly supportive and treated me very differently, for the better, when I transitioned. Bob, with whom I had worked closely and saw as a friend, barely ever spoke to me again, except as needed for work. Paul was concerned I might be gay. After I reassured him I was neither interested in him nor thought this was right for others, over time, he accepted it. Neal, who had avoided eye contact with me before, greeted me like I was his long-lost friend. Shawn, who was a friendly gay neighbor, began avoiding me when he found out I'd transitioned when I mentioned helping someone else with their issues. I bought a trans magazine at a bookstore in a small town. I was nervous about the clerk, a young guy who looked like he'd played linebacker on his high school football team. He instead was unexpectedly curious and positive about the whole thing. So, I never knew how people would respond, neither within expectations nor stereotypes.

But probably the most difficult to reconcile was my mother. When I proceeded toward transitioning at work, pre-op as is required under the internationally accepted standards of care, my mother was critical. She did not understand why I could not just be "me," cross-dressed, at home, but dress like a normal man when I went out in public. After all, "What will the neighbors think?" I wasn't particularly surprised, but I was disappointed. It seemed to me a particularly good way to develop some serious psychopathy. I explained to her that I had reached a point where I could not continue to live within the status quo of that phase of my life. I either had to transition, or I knew I would commit suicide. She begrudgingly tolerated and, I think, eventually accepted my transition. But I think it was important to her that I was still the same, funny (looking?) person she loved talking to and laughing with.

Although initially, my changing appearance made my brother uncomfortable, he was supportive throughout the process. Over time, he thought about and came to understand what I had gone through over the course of my life. We have a strong relationship to this day. My sister was not, initially, due to religious beliefs. She was initially horrified when I showed up for a visit to South America with my daughter, looking shapelier and prettier than she'd remembered. Ultimately, she came around with the books I provided and a realization that she didn't want me out of her life. My closest aunt and uncle, as well as my cousins, were supportive.

I had the support of my many trans friends to help me throughout the process, from the preliminary hormonal treatments and psychoanalysis through post-op recovery. I felt lucky. Many friends had no support, or even tolerance, from their families. Some had spouses or significant others who simply didn't know or knew and worked to tolerate the "behavior." Most who chose to transition did so single. It is simply much more complicated to be transgender or to transition without that support and acceptance. And I do not doubt that I would not be alive today without all of them.

I found the best mechanism for reticent people was to offer resources. Finding books that addressed my issues was especially helpful. I could provide copies to anyone seeking a better understanding of my circumstances or simply learning how to deal with me on a work or personal basis. My favorite transgender story, because, after all, doesn't everyone have one, was that of Jenny Garth, as described in her book She's Not There. She discusses her own youth, college, and early professional years through her transition. I related to almost every aspect of her life, the struggles she faced, and the evolution she went through to transition, as tremendous parallels existed in our lives (except my spouse divorced me). So, I bought multiple copies, gave them to family members, and offered them to coworkers and neighbors who expressed interest or reservations they sought to address. Some would accept, others wouldn't. I never forced the issue.

One of the more significant TCNE events I attended was the annual conference, First Event. It was a surprisingly large event, attended by many vendors and practitioners. It was how I found my therapist, a required multi-year element of the transitioning process, and how I met, evaluated, and ultimately chose a surgeon. By 2005, I had completed several years of therapy, as did my daughter, since my transition would have significant impacts on her. I completed the independent psychiatric assessment as well and was prepared for surgery. I traveled to Montreal to meet with the surgeon and plan which elements I would elect. Obviously, there is the reassignment via genitalia, but also consideration of Adam's Apple and breast augmentation.

Due to limited providers, the wait for surgical intervention can be lengthy, even after completion of the prerequisites. Fortunately for me, a cancellation occurred, and in February 2005, I returned to Montreal for two weeks for surgery and rehabilitation. A close friend so kindly drove me from Boston to Montreal, and another cared for my daughter while I was away. I remember awakening in excruciating pain, yet overjoyed that it was done. I was, however, frighteningly weak, such that staff at the rehab facility feared I might not recover or survive. The dilation process, bathing, and other daily routines were taxing. I recovered sufficiently to be released on schedule, and my friend returned to retrieve me.

The drive home from Montreal was excruciating. Despite being driven home in a Cadillac, I felt every bump, every pothole, every bridge joint, and every turn. I felt as though it set me back the whole two weeks of rehab. I barely left my bed for the first few days home. I followed medical instructions, though, and walked around the house the required number of times and hours per day. But I quickly realized I would never return to normal or work if I didn't push myself. So, the next day, I got up with the plan to walk to CVS, a little over a mile from home. It took me 45 minutes to walk past four houses to the corner. CVS was out of reach, but over the remaining two hours, I walked up the hill, past five houses, down two side streets, and back to the house. I completed a circle of about 400 yards in pain. I'd not achieved CVS, but it was a start.

The next day, I completed over a mile, in pain, but turned home short of CVS. I knew if I managed to get to CVS, I would not have the strength to make it home. But on the third day, I managed to make it to CVS. I bought a few badly needed items and made the trek home. The last few blocks pushed me a bit beyond my capabilities that day. But each day, pushing for more and farther cumulatively built up my strength and agility. It wasn't long before I was back to walking in heels.

Returning to work was largely uneventful. My coworkers had had several years to adjust, as a critical component of the process is to live in gender for a required period, contemporary with psychoanalysis and hormonal treatments. This period was crucial to ensuring I was on the appropriate path and understood transition would not resolve life's problems. I continued to attend events and see my friends. Most importantly to me, I continued raising my daughter. So, appropriately, almost nothing about transitioning during the post-surgical phase was memorable.

I did have a few particularly hurtful experiences post-surgery. My job involved on-site work at firms my agency oversaw. On one occasion, in Ohio, staff had apparently been advised that a transexual woman would be working there. Mid-morning the first day, I went to the ladies' room, where a woman was ranting about how disgusting it was and worse that they had to share the bathroom with such a sick person. Ironically, she didn't even realize I was the sick person she was ranting about, but it hurt nonetheless. Reminding myself that she was narrow-minded and bigoted was little consolation. On another occasion, I was in Atlanta for work, staying at the hotel where Southern Comfort, a large transgender event I had not attended that year, was held the prior week. I ate dinner at the bar, and a man started a conversation with me and eventually insisted I was "one of them." I was incredulous. Why engage at all if he had a problem with people like me? He just wanted to cause trouble, no doubt, and I bet I can guess who he'll be voting for this November. There were a few other similar incidents over the years, but I've learned to redirect it as their problem, not mine.

When I did have to travel overnight for work, my daughter would stay with one of two families of her friends. Sometimes, she just wanted to be home, and I had several friends who would gladly stay with her till I returned home. Two were less enthusiastic once they met our ghosts. David had the intimidating habit of standing at the foot of the bed, visible only in silhouette but for his eyes. But that's an entirely different story.

Two years after surgery, I received several promotions, in succession, that sent me to work in Washington, DC. My daughter was in high school. The two families both offered to have her stay with them so she could finish high school there. I offered her the option, as it was a top-rated school system. She declined. She was ready to see what else the world had to offer. But I wanted her to get the best education possible, so I let her pick where we'd look to move. She researched the quality of schools in various commutable areas for me, based on things like SAT scores and percentage college matriculation. We ended up in suburban Maryland. We left our friends behind and began to make new friends. My daughter quickly made friends and became immersed in our new home's school and social scene.

There was no organization like TCNE there. Worse, I was very passable. Before long, I had left the transgender community behind. I was 40 going on 22. I longed for the experiences I had missed out on as a young woman. So, while my daughter was consumed by her friends and boyfriend (mainly once she had her driver's license), We lived near the mall and several restaurants and bars. I met lots of single and divorced men. I also met a woman, and it nearly went somewhere, but her own daughter wasn't comfortable with the relationship.

Eventually, one of those men got serious, and we eventually got engaged and moved in together. In the long run, it proved a mistake, but it seemed a romantic dream at the time. We were two very different people, and part of his motivation was financial. I was pretty successful by then and well paid. I afforded him a lifestyle he couldn't achieve on his own. In retrospect, he had had a habit of dating women for lifestyle, particularly after his two divorces. But he was also financially irresponsible. His car was repossessed one night because he'd stopped making car payments. It was an early warning sign for what was to come, but I chose to overlook it to give him a chance to redeem himself.

He did not. It became increasingly evident he had an alcohol use disorder. Two years later, he could not renew his license due to unpaid child support (all his sons were well into adulthood by this time). I helped him get on a payment plan and get his license back. He could then no longer afford to contribute to rent. Six months later, there was an issue with an insurance lapse, and he could not renew his pickup truck's registration. And then, finally, one of his grandnieces precipitated a fight in which I discovered, after more than three years, they were his granddaughters. With his brother's wife. During his first marriage. That ended it.

I went on a scattered handful of dates over the next five years, but from happenstance meetings with men, I hit it off with. It's particularly easy when you understand how they think. I've seen men from both sides. Sometimes, this makes me overly empathetic to men who struggle to meet someone. Once, while traveling, I set myself up for a sexual assault. I went through just sickening self-loathing, questioning every decision I made that evening, blaming myself for putting myself in that situation. It took about two years for me to stop blaming myself. But like many women, I was raised with the adage, "Any girl who gets raped did something to deserve it." I took psychology and sociology courses in college that taught me better. Yet still, the self-blame. My mother rued the day she last uttered that in front of me. Assault is not unlike losing a loved one, and it takes time to work through the emotions, the grief, and the regrets. And with time, I did.

I haven't dated since before the pandemic. Men still give me their phone numbers, and I take them kindly, but as I explain, I am seldom in any one place for long. I have chosen a nomadic life, ironically perhaps, since my international high school's yearbook was called "Nomad." Occasionally, there is a desire for companionship, but it passes, and I accept my life as it is now. It is not perfect by any means. Everyday struggles everyone encounters ensure that. Compromised credit cards, broken appliances, flat tires, allergies, colds, COVID-19, the flu, deaths in the family, executing the estates, and more intrude on a routine basis. Transitioning didn't solve that.

In fact, transitioning is an isolating experience. While my pre-op friends looked to me for advice and inspiration, post-operation, while I could relate to past experiences, I was in a new phase of life and experiences. I was on a new journey to which they could not relate. Likewise, with my transgender friends for whom transition was not an option. I remained close with many until we moved to DC. I had no transgender contacts there, nor did I want any. I wanted to live and be perceived as a "normal" woman. It is difficult to do that hanging out with transgender friends, especially if they don't pass well.

The ciswomen I am friends with simply assume I've had similar experiences with dating and men, menstruation and pregnancy, and menopause. But I don't relate, much as they could not relate to my experiences. You feel a bit like an imposter, but from experience, you know you can be sincere and have those friends. And you end up with few friends. Womanhood is hard fought and hard won by women; that is equally, but differently, true for transgender women. And the tearing down of women by women that we have all seen is one reason not to be open about our origin stories.

On the plus side, I sometimes use my man voice over the phone to get better service and be taken seriously. So, there's that…

-Poppy DeKenney

Part Two:

Parental Estrangement

The people referenced here have not been named for their own privacy. It is my story, not theirs. They have a right to have their say if they choose to.

I stared at my phone screen, paralyzed, frozen, unable to move, breathe or speak. There was an eerie silence in my head as I looked at the words from a text message:

"I'd like my things from the house; what day suits you?"

On the surface, it was a polite request to organize the collection of some things. I could not function because the words were from my son, the center of my Universe, my only child, my reason for being.

My paralysis came from the half-expected but still horribly hurtful feeling of finality that there was no more hope. No more hope of a return, a reconciliation, restorative justice, peace, happiness, unicorns and rainbows.

There was no "Hi Mum; I'd love to collect my things from home please, when suits you best?" or "Hi Mum, love you, time to collect my clutter <smiley face>, can you give me a hand please when works for you?" or something like that.

My son left after yet another domestic volcano three years ago and never returned. He turned up on the doorstep of a family member who no longer speaks to me.

I made a vow to myself a few weeks ago that I would never shed another tear over any man again. The mantra started out as "that man" and then turned into "any man." I might even change it to "anyone." It was a promise to myself that I would not allow other people to upset me, hurt me, or cause me anxiety, distress, or emotional pain.

How did I go from being a very grounded, happy, organized, independent, kind, loving, happy, together person to being a broken, shattered, hurtful, spiteful, angry, damaged, hateful, cold person?

I asked myself the same question over and over again, "Who stole my life?"

I know that when I start asking that question, I am in a high victim mindset. I switch from victim to martyr. My martyr mode is when I start finishing sentences with "............................ for you." I did that for you; after all I did for you, I gave up this activity for you, and this is how you treat me. Blah blah.

I feel like I have spent the last 5 years crying nonstop, and I can't even blame Covid for that.

Thirty-two years ago, my beautiful son came into this world—an unplanned but welcome surprise. I was married to his father at the time, and things were good. I had it all - on paper only - because I was desperately unhappy deep down. My beautiful son was born in the early 90's. At that time, I did not have a house phone, driving license, mobile phone, or access to the internet. If I wanted to make a phone call, I had to run up the road to the pay phone and hope for the best. I laugh about this now, but that was my usual.

Early on, it became clear that he was not developing as he should have been, and spent a long time in and out of the hospital. We saw every specialist available, every "ologist," every specialty beginning with psy. No one was ever able to truly offer a diagnosis other than delayed development and a congenital neurological sporadic mutation.

Eventually, at age 30, he received a diagnosis of Level 3 autism. I have always known he has autism; getting a diagnosis simply took a long time. He has always been different, marginalized, segregated, protected, guarded, enabled, facilitated; some might even say mollycoddled. He is an only child; parents of only children tend to over-compensate, and I was a single parent for a long time.

The relationship with my son's father broke down when he was about five. We had been married for a while but divorced many years later.

For a time, parenting was shared, and then I took things over and became a solo parent with 100% responsibility for my son. It secretly suited me; I was no longer accountable to someone else. I relied heavily on my family, sisters, and mum for support. My father died not long after I split from my son's father. We were in a bubble. I was at the helm, organized everything, was the project manager, and things were done my way.

Being a single parent makes relationships challenging. Not everyone wants the added responsibility of an existing child, and for me, getting out the front door was a challenge in itself. I had a few long-term relationships, but none had worked out.

About seven years ago, I decided to give it one last go and made a decision to start dating again, with the full support of my son. I entertained him with silly anecdotes of my dates, and we always laughed about things. Six years ago, I met someone that caught my eye. He also had older children and understood some of the challenges of solo parenting.

We dated for a while, and things became serious early on. We both felt that we had a few miles on the clock. What was the point of dilly-dallying? He had a good relationship with my son at this stage, and we agreed to marry with everyone's blessing.

So far, so good. We had spent the previous Christmas together in a beautiful cottage in a rural location. It was perfect, everything I had ever wanted. It was a quiet family gathering with no pressure, no noise, no chaos, healthy food, an open fire, and lots of hugs and laughter. There was no reason to think the following Christmas would be different.

Tensions and power dynamics can be insidious. They can sneak up on you, inch by inch. Slowly, the joy and laughter in my home began to lessen, and I noticed that my new partner was being overly hard on my son and my son was being overly annoying. I was constantly stuck in the middle of their testosterone-driven disputes.

Son was used to having 100% of my attention 100% of the time. We had a structure, a routine, a life, a friendship. In hindsight, it was too insular. I did not see it at the time, but my partner did and just went about things in a rather horrible way.

Partner is in the armed forces and comes from a very male-dominated childhood of immense trauma. His methodology for imparting learning is to metaphorically bash the other person over the head until they get it right. My methodology is never to allow others to make mistakes and always do things for them.

Initially, my son enjoyed the structure and routine, but it became harder and harder to maintain. The pressure mounted, the expectations increased, and the stress levels climbed. There was explosion after explosion.

My partner stepped in as the disciplinarian and would chastise me for not having consequences for bad behavior. I repeatedly asked him to stay in his lane, but he failed dismally. If I agreed with my husband, my son would accuse me of bullying and get my family on board to support him. They would then relish ringing me up to yell at me. If I agreed with my son, my husband would feel undermined and yell at me. It's challenging to discipline an adult. He was a bit big to put under my arm and put on the naughty step even harder as I live in a bungalow.

My mental health was at an all-time low. I could not breathe. I could not function in my own home. My family was facilitating by allowing my son to stay with them sometimes to give me some head space, but when I look back, I think this might have made things worse. But I felt that my son needed a safe space, and it was no longer safe for him in his own home.

My husband would insist that everyone was facilitating bad behavior. Whenever one of us would get annoyed with my son, he would make contact with one of my family members and moan about us. Then, the family would invite him over.

We had yet another explosion in mid-December a few years ago. As always, we booked an Airbnb. My son and I had been doing that for quite some time. It was our thing, our time together, our escape from the madness, and we had shared this with my husband.

Things were tense before we left; in hindsight, we should never have gone. We were minding a dog at the time. We arrived at our Airbnb in separate vehicles. I had my son and the dog. My partner came on his own. I left the room to do something and heard the most unmerciful banging and shouting. I came out, and my partner was yelling at my son, threatening him with arrest, and throwing his things into his bag. My son went nuts, understandably, and jumped on his back. The rest is a blur. I flung my son's stuff in his bag and drove down the road with him; I had no idea where I was going. The dog was at the Airbnb and I could not leave him there. Oddly, I cared more about the dog than my partner. I sobbed and sobbed. That was Christmas morning. My partner had forbidden any gift exchanges. He wanted to give me gifts and nothing for my son. He wanted to ignore my son entirely and spend time with me. I could not have coped with that. He yelled at me that if we had done things his way, none of this would have happened.

He had already confiscated my son's phone and given him a regular, old-fashioned Nokia. Understandably, my son's nerves were a bit strained.

My partner asked my son to close the door, and the partner did not see the dog walking through at the time. My son probably gave a smart answer; my partner reacted (way way way too much testosterone). My son pushed my partner against a wall, and my partner reacted the way he did. I cannot confirm or deny this since I was in the next room.

I jumped into my car and drove like a crazy person down the road and rang one of my family members on the way who lived close by. I turned up on their doorstep sobbing on Christmas morning, interrupting their day, ditched my son and his belongings, and went back to rescue the dog. I genuinely did not care about my partner at this stage. I often wonder if I should have taken the dog with me and never have been seen again.

The situation grew worse and worse, with the partner eventually reporting my son for violent behavior. He wanted to put him into care. He wanted him arrested. He wanted him sued for defamation. The list went on. Finally, the partner decided to engage social services as my son is technically a vulnerable adult, and he felt made vulnerable by a vulnerable adult. The outcome of their findings was nil, but yet another nail had been hammered into the coffin of my relationship with my son.

I could go on and on with minute details about how things all fell apart, but the final straw was when my son hit my partner with his mobile phone because it was after mobile phone curfew. My partner yelled at my son to put his phone away. Partner insisted that son put his phone away at 10 pm each evening but would continue doom scrolling himself. My son understandably pushed back, and my partner restrained him, bruising. My family wanted my partner arrested, and I wanted to die.

My family whisked my son away and started passing him around between themselves. He was having so much fun that I no longer existed. I really struggled with this and still do. I tried to encourage my son to want to spend time with me. Still, it becomes a metaphorical "mummy and daddy fighting" scenario, and children become highly manipulative and use this to their advantage.

The frustration and anger that people I care about so much would hurt me in this way became unbearable, and I began to drink heavily. All I managed to achieve by this self-sabotaging behavior was to isolate my son even further and give everyone else another reason to remind me I was an unfit parent.

It is right to ask why I stayed in the situation for as long as I did and currently still am. I ask this of myself every day. Love is a funny emotion; it supersedes all other emotions and is the highest level of vibrational energy. I love my son, and I love my husband. I loved the man I thought I married; I love that husband, that version of him and that version of me that wanted the dream, the life, the family, the togetherness, the support, and the future. Many times, I have expressed my sadness and unhappiness, and many times, I am talked out of leaving, reminded of the promises I made and that my responsibility as a parent ended when my son became an adult. I have to disagree with the last bit. Children grow up and make new lives, but parents will always be parents, and sometimes relationships don't work.

Insights in no particular order of importance or insightfulness:

I was an enabler. I enabled my son's bad behavior by not encouraging him to be more independent. I always overcompensated for my perceived failure as a parent. I did too much for him; I never gave him space to breathe and never let him fail.

As a parent, your child will always be your child, but their perception of the relationship changes as they grow and become adults.

I know I felt and still do feel entitled to know what my son is up to, where he is, who he is living with, where he has gone on holidays, etc., but he is an adult, and I need to back off. It's hard knowing that my family is colluding; they do not see it this way.

Answers will come to you if you allow them and avoid clouding your judgment with substances. The answer is not at the bottom of a bottle unless that bottle is water.

You are your own rescue. There is no magic wand, no magic solution, no external force from above. The rescue may come from outside sources by helping you see through the fog, but ultimately, you can and will find the strength to cut through the noise and move forward. By putting your own happiness and mental health at the top of your priority list, you will come out the other side and not be afraid of what that looks like.

Keep a diary as an aide memoir; it will help you track how far you have come.

Take photos of yourself at your absolute worst. It might sound mad, but it will also help you see how far you have come and where you never want to go again.

Be mindful that you are vulnerable. I spent so much money on feng shui experts, manifestation courses, prayers, energy work, counseling, rubbish online courses offering law of attraction miracles, etc. Counseling, prayer, and energy work are powerful and have a place supporting your mental health, but I was highly vulnerable. I was approaching these supports from a place of desperation and fear, not acceptance and allowing.

Strategies that work for me:

If you feel like you are losing your reason, you probably are, and it's okay to reach out for support. I probably had two breakdowns and found the courage to reach out for some professional mental health support.

Structure gives me freedom. I have an appointment in my diary daily to go to the gym. It's my happy space. For 30 - 40 minutes, I can healthily externalize my inner pain, AND I get to have a fabulously long, hot, uninterrupted shower in a bathroom I don't have to clean.

I am mindful of who I am listening to and what I am listening to. I allowed too many people to have opinions on how I should be doing things. I stopped listening to outside influences and started listening to positive stuff instead. I now listen to audiobooks, things that make me laugh, podcasts, meditations, basically anything and everything that nourishes and nurtures my brain. A close friend introduced me to Neville Goddard and also to this book. For that, I am eternally grateful.

I started to wear make-up daily, even if I was not going out - you never know - the postman might want to go on a date at 8 am. That was not about feeling like I was hiding behind a mask; I decided I wanted to like what I saw in the mirror and stop frightening the horses. I began to feel better about myself because I looked better.

I have also written rather long-winded, cathartic letters to my family. I may shred them. It allowed me to pour my heart out in a safe way.

I journal daily. Sometimes, it's an intention-setting exercise; sometimes, it's a brain dump/rant. I have started journaling daily. At first, I always felt that journaling was a bit lame, but now I realize it is about having somewhere to go with your thoughts. I brain dump at the end of the day most days and set some intentions in the mornings.

At the time of writing, the situation remains unresolved. I have updated my Will and written a rather lengthy Letter of Wishes. That has no legal standing, but it indicates to my executors what I would like to happen. That gives me mental peace.

Parental estrangement is horrible. It happens for various reasons. For some odd reason, the power dynamic now shifts to the child, and the parent is the one doing all the running. No one can ever change the biological relationship between a parent and a child. No one is responsible for anyone else's happiness other than their own. Find something good to focus on daily, and surround yourself with positive people, beautiful things, thoughts, and inspiring energy. Celebrate every day - aging is a privilege, and so is parenting.

Some books that helped me:

Psycho Cybernetics - Maxwell Maltz

Rules of Estrangemenet - Joshua Coleman

Done with the crying - Sheri McGregor

Imagination creates reality - Neville Goddard

Letter to myself

Dear gorgeous you -

By the time you read this, you will have reconciled with your gorgeous son, you will be involved in his life, and he will be living his own life on his terms.

You have sorted things out with your now ex-husband. He has left your life with compassion and empathy, and you have forgiven each other for what has happened. When you married him, you loved him, and a part of you will always love him, but the relationship came at such a high cost that it was not worth it.

Your life is calmer now; your mental health has improved dramatically. You look and feel so much better, and you feel lighter and younger.

You have used your writing to move yourself forward. You are working 100% remotely, allowing you to move into The Castle with your true soul mate. He has patiently waited for you, and you for him. You were meant for each other when you met 25 years ago.

You genuinely love yourself and have so much love to give and receive. You have healed your heart.

Your daily actions keep you grounded. You go to the gym daily, meditate, and pray daily. You prioritize you.

You almost burst with pride at your son's graduation. You've got this, and the Universe has you.

All my love for you. You matter.

x

Dear estranged child -

Whatever reason you have for distancing yourself from your parent, know that your parent is in incredible pain, and maybe this decision was right for you at that time.

I ask you to reach out, make amends, seek forgiveness, and seek reconciliation. Life is short. We only regret the things we do not do.

Know that you are loved; know that you are wanted. Know that you have a parent or parents that love you and always will. Expect miracles.

From an estranged parent

THIS IS FOR YOU

To the mothers who sacrificed so much
that a part of themselves
became the core of us.
To the mothers who worried through the night,
arose before the sun
and dressed us with affection.
To the mothers never resting.
To the mothers pinching pennies.
To the mothers juggling impossible odds nonchalantly.
To the mothers burnt from both ends and running out of
wick.
This is for you.
To the mothers who dropped their own dreams
and devoted their lives
to ours.
To the mothers who fought silent wars
never spoken of.
To the mothers who stitched and sewed,
worked themselves to the bone,
kept our stomachs and souls full,
and turned ordinary spaces
into warm-hearted homes.
To the mothers too hard on themselves.
To the mothers underappreciated.
To the mothers raising gentle beasts.
To the mothers raising compassionate warriors.
To the mothers raising conquering heroes.
This is for you.
To the mother hens and momma bears, you dare not cross.
To the mothers who cheered loudest when we won
and loved harder
when we lost.

To the mothers who wore every uniform,
carried us, cradled us, comforted us,
fueled our fiery dreams,
directed and captured our most cherished memories.
Pinned Polaroids across our hearts,
sent us out into a cold world
armed with graceful strength,
and waited anxiously for the phone to ring.
To the mothers who left the door open.
To the mothers who pray aloud for us.
To the mothers still waiting.
This is for you.
To the mothers whose lessons linger like fingerprints,
we'll make you proud.
To the mothers whose voices still echo through us,
we'll turn your words into music.
To the mothers who made us into artwork,
we're creating a beautiful life
in your honor.
This,
all of this,
is for you.
Jack Raymond

-Anonymous

Hello to all readers. I am Singha. I hope you all read and liked my letters in previous books. Now, I am back again with another true experience of my life.

It was tough for me as a teenager and as a child as well. I am the second child of my parents. I heard my mother saying in my childhood that they never wanted me as a second child, but because of the pressure of their parents (my grandparents), they felt forced to have another child. I was born nine years after my elder brother was born. Initially, it was not felt by me, but as I grew up, I started noticing that there was favoritism for my brother. He was given the best of everything, like food and clothing, and I had to wait for my school uniform. I was angry and sad; it had a terrible effect on me, and later, when I grew up, they stopped financing my education and my pocket money, so I had to leave my home and stop learning. I started working in an ashram and learning the techniques of yoga and meditation with breathing exercises.

It was an excellent experience for me to stay in an ashram. I learned so much during that time and became such a good person. I cut contact with my parents, and they also stopped all communication with me. Before I joined the ashram, I was an alcoholic because I was depressed and frustrated, and I had so much anger toward my parents and my elder brother. He used to abuse me verbally and physically when I was a child. He never let me touch his things. If I did, he used to hit me. That was such a punishment and trauma for me. I carried that trauma until I was 22. After going to the ashram, I started working on healing my past traumas with the help of my teacher. He is such a saint; he is an awakened spiritual human being. I am very grateful to God that he chose me as one of his disciples, taught me yoga and meditation, and helped me to heal all my traumas.

I am sharing my experience because I want to give some confidence to people going through the same issue. I know it's easy to say to forgive, but it's hard to be the one to do it. But believe me, that's the only way to cure the trauma and become a peaceful human being. Our parents are not God; they are human beings. Yes, I agree they must treat children equally and not abuse them, but I would like to convey my message: hate and anger only bring bad energy to you. Currently, I am 34, and I don't have any anger and hate for my parents and brother. I realized it's part of their karma, but what's in my control is the ability to come out from the trauma and become a good person who loves and cares for others and society.

-Singha

Dear Self,

Regret is a heavy emotion. It weighs you down like being under deep water. You feel the weight all around you, but you want to breathe anyway. You know that doing so will end painfully. You just keep holding your breath.

Dad was never my enemy. He was just a casualty of bad situations and life choices. Now, sitting here, watching the birds eat from the feeders, regret clouds my thinking.

The truth is, I don't know if Dad is alive or dead. I do know I was never anything he would ever be proud of. I never fit in his world. I never wanted to fit in his world.

Can you imagine me in a dress and heels? Can you imagine me drinking socially and saying polite little quips that never offend anyone? Or can you picture me saying veiled words with nuanced meanings? I laugh thinking about it. Eventually, a "Fuck you" would have slipped out. It would have been inevitable.

Still, I wonder if I did the right thing by not reconnecting with him when our brother and sister did. Not making my child 'get to know him.' Right, nope, that is not the real truth. I never forced our family on my son. He was allowed to skip any family social occasion he wanted to. Part of that was Dad. I remember how he would say, "This is a family event. You will go, and you will behave like a family!" I hated that. We were not a family. Mom was batshit bananas, and Dad had a mean violent streak. Not as violent as Mom, but it was there.

I remember him throwing my brother down the hall like a football. My brother was all of five years old when it happened. His body just went down the hall, crashing into the walls and bouncing off the doors. Why? I still don't remember why.

Mom would beat the hell out of us way worse than Dad. Yet here she is, squatting in my life like some sick, rabid dog. I could at least walk away from Dad. I have not talked to him since I turned 18, and he no longer had to pay child support.

That was the heart of the matter. Money. As long as we cost him money he had to deal with us. When he did not pay, we were not important. That is not all the truth. That is too easy a lie to flip around as an excuse.

The truth is, dear self, I walked away. I chose never to associate with him. I would have chosen never to associate with the psycho bitch either, but again money conflicted life.

It is easy to lay the blame at a bad parent's feet. It is easy to place the burden of right and wrong on their shoulder. It is way harder to be a Christian. It is harder to wonder if I should open the door again and try to find out if he is alive. To seek him out and ask for forgiveness.

Yeah, I know that sounds strange. Because everything in me says he deserves to be gone and that he was bad, but don't get me wrong, he was not great. He was bad. He just was not as bad as I built him up to be. I chose to walk away. I chose to leave him. I chose never to forgive. I chose never to understand. I chose to harden my heart. Because at the end of the day, I became an adult and behaved like a child.

I didn't acknowledge that I used him and Mom to behave badly. That I did really stupid and bad things. Then said, "Oh, it was just my upbringing. Not my fault at all." Excuses are not in the best interest of the Christian path.

He was violent, he was manipulative, and he was human. He was probably selfish. At the end of the day, though, dearest self. He did not leave me. He never walked away. He tried to stay. He at least made a small, weak attempt to try. At the end of the day, it was I who walked away. It was me who shut the door. It was I who had the unforgiving and merciless heart. And so, I have the weight of regret drowning me.

It is I who need to ask for forgiveness for being weak.

Many would say I was right. Many would say it was wise. They would say my parents were abusive and toxic. They would be right. However, the path to redemption is sometimes more complex than ever imagined. If your daughter cannot forgive you, how can you be forgiven?

Do we have to engage in an active relationship again? Honestly, it is too late. I do need to ask for forgiveness for my selfish, hard heart. Perhaps, if instead of blaming Dad for all my faults, I accepted responsibility for my actions…things would be different now. Dad was not my enemy. He was just a man who was….not ideal. He was cruel. He did things that were beyond hurtful. He was incapable of being better than he was.

So was I. The difference became that I really began to believe in Jesus. I believe his way is the right path. It is not an easy path. I sometimes regret taking it. Especially when I face such questions as this. Do I try to contact Dad and ask for forgiveness? Do I acknowledge I was wrong for giving up? Do I finally accept the actions that I did during that time? Do I take responsibility for the things I did? Things I have not even written about in this letter because I am still a coward?

It is a good thing I am a Christian. Because Jesus knows I am not strong enough to deal with this. I will continue not to know if he is alive or dead because I am just not strong enough. I am just surprised I was strong enough to walk down this path of shadowed thinking.

I love you now, self. You are a messed-up bundle of philosophical self-reflection. Now stop thinking about this, or you will never get to sleep! Just wake up tomorrow and do better, okay?

Sincerely

Yourself

-Elizabeth Myers

Part Three:
Parental Alienation

The Loss of my Kids

I'm a father of five children, and I have three women that carried them. You know, like every relationship, they start off great, etc.

Well, with my first wife, I had two children. My wife and I started at the age of 14; we had our first son at eighteen. We were still kids ourselves, but you know how you stick in there for the love of the child who didn't ask to be here. Now, I was trying to figure out life. You go on a run for six and a half years of ups and downs, trying to stay strong, but you can sense that the end is coming, and then pops up another child: a girl. So, we have to put another bandage on the situation. So, I stuck around for another six months. Finally, I was saying this will not work and the funny thing is that she didn't want it to work. Since we were both ready for the end of the relationship, you would think it would be an easy split, but nope! Here comes the vindictive and spiteful way. Wait, to take you back for a second with my first son. Times got really bad, so I sent my son to live with my mom because I thought my wife at the time was out of her mind. With her knowing what she put me through, you would think there was a clear understanding, but nope! As I said, I left, but I still wanted to see my daughter. So, in many situations, you have a young or old lady who wants to have her cake and eat it, too. Meaning she wants another life with you, but that can't be the case. Me I would like to come pick up my daughter. So, one of the first times, I got there to pick up my daughter, and she knew I was coming, but my daughter wasn't ready. So, I find that unbelievable, but for my ex, that was just an "I want to make you mad tactic." I finally got the BS situated that one time. After that, it was an onslaught of issues, like, "No, you can't see her," and a host of more BS. I'm talking about fighting with her family and friends, courts, supervised visits, and also me only being able to see my daughter once a week for eight hours.

Talk about pissed! I felt like I was losing my mind, and this was never going to stop. So, I gathered my thoughts together. I am going through a severe mental breakdown, but every day, I am picking myself up. Saying it only gets better from here. So, I went through the tough time and then had to start putting the right things in place. I would say that being transparent with myself and others began to help me through the journey. So, I found truly genuine people, and I told my story. With that, you get great feedback and advice. The main thing is keeping the main thing, which is my child. It all starts and ends with you. Take care and love yourself, and the love will help you; love and see the light at the end of the tunnel, and there is a light. Trust and believe. They can only put up the front for so long. Okay, back to the main thing: the child. They can see the light in you and the love in you, which gives you the upper hand because now you have the child fighting with you against the forces (the woman). Stay strong and stay focused, fellas!

-Jayson Fieldings, Sr.

APPENDIX ON SUPPORT RESOURCES & CHOICES

Includes Links, Numbers, & Resources For LGBTQIA+, Parental Estrangement, & Parental Alienation

LGBTQIA+:

https://glaad.org/resourcelist/

https://www.thetrevorproject.org/resources/

https://lgbthotline.org/

https://itgetsbetter.org/

https://gaycenter.org

https://www.gmhc.org

transgenderlawcenter.org

Parental Estrangement:

https://lifestance.com

https://locator.apa.org/

NAMI Helpline (National Alliance on Mental Illness) 1-800-950-6264

APPENDIX ON SUICIDE RESOURCES

Includes Resources for
Suicide Help & Assessment

List of Suicide Help & Hotlines[1]:
(United States and Worldwide)

United States:
Emergency: 911
Suicide Hotline: 988

Algeria:
Emergency: 34342 and 43
Suicide Hotline: 0021 3983 2000 58

Angola:
Emergency: 113

Argentina:
Emergency: 911
Suicide Hotline: 135

Armenia:
Emergency: 911 and 112

---

[1] List of Helplines and Hotline Numbers Retrieved from blog.opencounseling.com

Suicide Hotline: (2) 538194

Australia:
Emergency: 000
Suicide Hotline: 131114

Austria:
Emergency: 112
Telefonseelsorge 24/7 142
Rat auf Draht 24/7 147 (Youth)

Bahamas:
Emergency: 911
Suicide Hotline: (2) 322-2763

Bahrain:
Emergency: 999

Bangladesh:
Emergency: 999

Barbados:
Emergency: 911
Suicide Hotline Samaritan Barbados: (246) 4299999

Belgium:
Emergency: 112
Suicide Hotline Stichting Zelfmoordlijn: 1813

Bolivia:
Emergency: 911
Suicide Hotline: 3911270

Bosnia & Herzegovina:
Suicide Hotline: 080 05 03 05

Botswana:
Emergency: 911
Suicide Hotline: +2673911270

Brazil:
Emergency: 188

Bulgaria:
Emergency: 112
Suicide Hotline: 0035 9249 17 223

Burundi:
Emergency: 117

Burkina Faso:
Emergency: 17

Canada:
Emergency: 911
Suicide Hotline: 1 (822) 456 4566

Chad:
Emergency: 2251-1237

China:
Emergency: 110
Suicide Hotline: 800-810-1117

Columbia:
24/7 Helpline in Barranquilla: 1(00 57 5) 372 27 27

24/7 Hotline Bogota: (57-1 323 24 25

Congo:
Emergency: 117

Costa Rica:
Emergency: 911
Suicide Hotline: 506-253-5439

Croatia:
Emergency: 112

Cyprus:
Emergency: 112
Suicide Hotline: 8000 7773

Czech Republic:
Emergency: 112

Denmark:
Emergency: 112
Suicide Hotline: 4570201201

Dominican Republic:
Emergency: 911
Suicide Hotline: (809) 562-3500

Ecuador:
Emergency: 911

Egypt:
Emergency: 122
Suicide Hotline: 131114

El Salvador:
Emergency: 911
Suicide Hotline: 126

Equatorial Guinea:
Emergency: 114

Estonia:
Emergency:112
Suicide Hotline: 3726558088
In Russian: 3726555688

Ethiopia:
Emergency: 911

Finland:
Emergency: 112
Suicide Hotline: 010 195 202

France:
Emergency: 112
Suicide Hotline: 0145394000

Germany:
Emergency: 112
Suicide Hotline: 0800 111 0 111

Ghana:
Emergency: 999
Suicide Hotline: 2332 444 71279

Greece:
Emergency: 1018

Guatemala:
Emergency: 110
Suicide Hotline: 5392-5953

Guinea:
Emergency: 117

Guinea Bissau:
Emergency: 117

Guyana:
Emergency: 999
Suicide Hotline: 223-0001

Holland:
Suicide Hotline: 09000767

Hong Kong:
Emergency: 999
Suicide Hotline: 852 2382 0000

Hungary:
Emergency: 112
Suicide Hotline: 116123

India:
Emergency: 112
Suicide Hotline: 8888817666

Indonesia:
Emergency: 112
Suicide Hotline: 1-800-273-8255

Iran:
Emergency: 110
Suicide Hotline: 1480

Ireland:
Emergency: 116123
Suicide Hotline: +4408457909090

Israel:
Emergency: 100
Suicide Hotline: 1201

Italy:
Emergency: 112
Suicide Hotline: 800860022

Jamaica:
Suicide Hotline: 1-888-429-KARE (5273)

Japan:
Emergency: 110
Suicide Hotline: 810352869090

Jordan:
Emergency: 911
Suicide Hotline: 110

Kenya:
Emergency: 999
Suicide Hotline: 722178177

Kuwait:
Emergency: 112
Suicide Hotline: 94069304

Latvia:
Emergency: 113
Suicide Hotline: 371 67222922

Lebanon:
Suicide Hotline: 1564

Liberia:
Emergency: 911
Suicide Hotline: 6534308

Luxembourg:
Emergency: 112
Suicide Hotline: 352 45 45 45

Madagascar:
Emergency: 117

Malaysia:
Emergency: 999
Suicide Hotline: (06) 2842500

Mali:
Emergency: 8000-1115

Malta:
Suicide Hotline: 179

Mauritius:
Emergency: 112
Suicide Hotline: +230 800 93 93

Mexico:
Emergency: 911
Suicide Hotline: 5255102550

Netherlands:
Emergency: 112
Suicide Hotline: 900 0113

New Zealand:
Emergency: 111
Suicide Hotline: 1737

Niger:
Emergency: 112

Nigeria:
Suicide Hotline: 234 8092106493

Norway:
Emergency: 112
Suicide Hotline: +4781533300

Pakistan:
Emergency: 115

Peru:
Emergency: 911
Suicide Hotline: 381-3695

Philippines:
Emergency: 911
Suicide Hotline: 028969191

Poland:
Emergency: 112
Suicide Hotline: 5270000

Portugal:
Emergency: 112
Suicide Hotline: 21 854 07 40
And 8 96 898 21 50

Qatar:
Emergency: 999

Romania:
Emergency: 112
Suicide Hotline: 0800 801200

Russia:
Emergency: 112
Suicide Hotline: 0078202577577

Saint Vincent and the Grenadines:
Suicide Hotline: 9784 456 1044

São Tomé and Príncipe:
Suicide Hotline: (239) 222-12-22 ext. 123

Saudi Arabia:
Emergency: 112

Serbia:
Suicide Hotline: (+381) 21-6623-393

Senegal:
Emergency: 17

Singapore:
Emergency: 999
Suicide Hotline: 1 800 2214444

Spain:
Emergency: 112
Suicide Hotline: 914590050

South Africa:
Emergency: 10111
Suicide Hotline: 0514445691

South Korea:
Emergency: 112
Suicide Hotline: (02) 7158600

Sri Lanka:
Suicide Hotline: 011 057 2222662

Sudan:
Suicide Hotline: (249) 11-555-253

Sweden:
Emergency: 112
Suicide Hotline: 46317112400

Switzerland:
Emergency: 112
Suicide Hotline: 143

Tanzania:
Emergency: 112

Thailand:
Suicide Hotline: (02) 713-6793

Tonga:
Suicide Hotline: 23000

Trinidad and Tobago:
Suicide Hotline: (868) 645 2800

Tunisia:
Emergency: 197

Turkey:
Emergency: 112

Uganda:
Emergency: 112
Suicide Hotline: 0800 21 21 21

United Arab Emirates:
Suicide Hotline: 800 46342

United Kingdom:
Emergency: 112
Suicide Hotline: 0800 689 5652

United States:
Emergency: 911
Suicide Hotline: 988

Zambia:
Emergency: 999
Suicide Hotline: +260960264040

Zimbabwe:
Emergency: 999
Suicide Hotline: 080 12 333 333

CONDUCT A SUICIDE INQUIRY[2]

a. Ideation

Frequency, Intensity and Duration

- Have you had thoughts of hurting yourself or others?
- Have you thought about ending your life?

Now, in the Past, and at its Worst

- During the last 48 hours, past month, and worst ever: How much? How intense? Lasting for how long?

b. Plan

Timing, Location, Lethality, Availability/Means

- When you think about killing yourself or ending your life, what do you imagine?
- When? Where? How would you do it? In what way?

---

[2] Retrieved from Minnesota Department of Health at: https://www.health.state.mn.us/people/syringe/suicide.pdf

Preparatory Acts

- What steps have you taken to prepare to kill yourself, if any?

c. Behavior

Past attempts, aborted attempts, rehearsals

- Have you ever thought about or tried to kill yourself in the past?
- Have you ever taken any actions to rehearse or practice ending your life (e.g., tying noose, loading gun, measuring substance)?

Non-suicidal self-injurious behavior

- Are you having paranoid thoughts? Hallucinations?
- Have you done anything to hurt yourself (e.g., cutting, burning or mutilation)?

d. Intent

Extent to which they expect to carry out the plan and believe the plan to be lethal versus harmful.

- What do you think will happen?
- What things put you at risk of ending your life or

killing yourself (reasons to die)?
- What things prevent you from killing yourself and keep you safe (reasons to live)?

Explore ambivalence between reasons to die and reasons to live. Pay attention to how they describe the outcome.

- "I'm dead, it's over." indicates a higher risk of suicide death.
- "I think I'd end up in the hospital." indicates a moderate risk of suicide death.
- "I don't want to die; I want my suffering to end." indicates a lower risk of suicide death.

e. Notes

- When working with **youth**, collect information from a parent, guardian or service provider on the youth's suicidal thoughts, plans, behaviors, and changes in mood, behavior or disposition.
- If the person has thoughts or plans to **harm someone else**, conduct a homicide inquiry using the same questions (replace "hurt or kill yourself" with "hurt or kill someone else").

DETERMINE RISK LEVEL[3]

The risk level is determined with the previous three steps:

1. Risk Factors
2. Protective Factors
3. Suicide Inquiry

Death by Suicide Risk Level

Risk Level	Risk Factors	Protective Factors	Suicide Inquiry	Intervention*
High	Multiple risk factors	Protective factors are not present or not relevant at this time	Potentially lethal suicide attempt or persistent ideation with strong intent or suicide rehearsal	Hospital admission generally indicated, suicide precautions (e.g., observation, means reduction)
Moderate	Multiple risk factors	Few protective factors	Suicidal ideation with a plan, but not intent or behavior	Hospital admission may be necessary, develop crisis plan and suicide precautions, give emergency/crisis numbers

---

[3] Retrieved from Minnesota Department of Health at: https://www.health.state.mn.us/people/syringe/suicide.pdf

Low	Few and/or modifiable risk factors	Strong protective factors	Thoughts of death with no plan, intent or behavior	Outpatient referral, symptom reduction, give emergency/crisis numbers

Take every suicide attempt seriously!
People often think a person is not really suicidal.
It's better to be safe, even if they will be angry with you for taking action to keep them alive.

ABOUT THE AUTHOR

Jen Taylor, LCSW
#1 International Bestselling Author

Jen Taylor, LCSW is a New York-based spiritual psychotherapist with 23+ years of experience. Jen specializes in womens' empowerment, domestic violence, teens, and LGBTQIA+ individuals. Jen incorporates spirituality and astrology into her sessions to create a truly unique blend of guidance.

Jen was born and raised in New York City and lived there from preschool through high school. Instead of attending her prom, Jen went to boot camp for the Navy and received accreditation as a U.S. Naval photographer. Jen then received her Bachelor's in Arts from Haverford College in Pennsylvania and studied abroad in Florence, Italy. She spent her early 20s in the advertising office of Italian *Vogue* and went on to attend social work school at Fordham University's Graduate school of social services. In 1999, Jen received her Master's in social work while pregnant with her first child, Giancarlo. Jen worked in various outpatient mental health clinics in New York City, and in 2007 had her second child, Elisabetta.

Jen Taylor, LCSW is the editor for Girl on Fire Magazine's "Wine Down with Jen," where she uses her 20+ years of experience as a New York-based spiritual psychotherapist to bring you cozy couch conversations you would have with your best friend over a glass of wine after work.

When not writing for the magazine or seeing clients, Jen enjoys traveling, photography, spending time with her kids, and a good cup of coffee.

Jen is a multiple #1 International bestselling author in a collaboration series and currently working on releasing the rest of this series as her very first solo books over the next year.

To connect with Jen, she can be reached at:

Jentaylorfani@gmail.com

www.ingramcontent.com/pod-product-compliance
Lightning Source LLC
LaVergne TN
LVHW051957060526
838201LV00059B/3692